101 one hundred one SIGNS of DESIGN

TIMELESS TRUTHS FROM GENESIS

101 *one hundred one* SIGNS *of* DESIGN

TIMELESS TRUTHS FROM GENESIS

KEN HAM

Master
Books

First printing: August 2002

ISBN: 0-89051-365-1
Library of Congress Catalog Card Number: 2002105384

Printed in the United States of America.
Please visit our website for other great titles:
www.masterbooks.net
For information regarding author interviews, please
contact the publicity department at (870) 438-5288.

one hundred one SIGNS of DESIGN

INTRODUCTION

In John 5: 45–47, Jesus Christ spoke these words:

> Do not think that I will accuse you to the Father: there is one that accuseth you, even Moses, in whom ye trust. For had ye believed Moses, ye would have believed me: for he wrote of me. But if ye believe not his writings, how shall ye believe my words?

The first book included in the writings of Moses is the Book of Genesis. Not only is this the first book in the entire Bible, it is also the most quoted-from or referred-to book in the whole of Scripture. This is not surprising, as Genesis, which means "origins," includes an account of the origin of all the basic entities of life and the universe. As such, it is the foundational book for the rest of the Bible.

Every biblical doctrine of theology, directly or indirectly, has its foundation in the history recorded in Genesis 1–11. If the history in Genesis is not true (and this history includes geology, biology, astronomy, anthropology, chemistry, and so on), then Christianity can't be true either.

The doctrine of marriage, for instance, including its intertwined links with the gospel, is based on the account of the creation of Adam and Eve. If the biology and anthropology of Genesis are not true, then the doctrine of marriage — the binding union of one man for one woman, as for Christ and His Bride, the Church — cannot be true either. This teaching is based on Adam being formed from dust and Eve from his side. All human beings descended from Adam, with Jesus Christ in His humanity becoming a descendant of Adam (called the "Last Adam").

As you read this book of quotes, I trust you will be challenged anew concerning the vital importance of accepting Genesis as literal history — just as it is written and was intended to be taken.

A number of Christian leaders have told me recently, "Genesis is just a metaphor." I reply that if Genesis is a metaphor, then what about the account of Adam and Eve? Well, "It's a metaphor," they answer. . . . All the genealogies show that Jesus Christ was a descendant of Adam. So are we to believe that real people go . . . *all the way back to a metaphor?*

2

The Bible is not just the
ultimate authority in all matters of faith and practice.
The Bible is the ultimate authority in all matters
of faith and practice and everything it touches upon
(which includes geology, biology, etc.).

Ultimately, the history in
Genesis 1—11 is foundational

to every single biblical doctrine of theology. Why did Jesus die on the cross? Why do we wear clothes? Why is there sin? Why is there death? Why is Jesus called the last Adam? Why does man have dominion? Why is there a doctrine of work? Why marriage? Why a seven-day week? All these doctrines are founded in Genesis 1–11.

Genesis is one of the most disbelieved and attacked books of the Bible in both Christian and non-Christian circles. Yet, Genesis is the most quoted book in the Bible.

Many church–going people appear to be ignorant of the fact that all Christian doctrine is founded in the Book of Genesis. Virtually every (some would say every) single doctrine of theology, directly or indirectly, has its foundation in the first book of the Bible.

6

Dinosaurs first existed around 6,000 years ago. *Because dinosaurs were land animals, and God made all the land animals on day 6 of the creation week, dinosaurs were created on day 6. Dinosaurs could not have died out before this time because death, bloodshed, disease, and suffering is a result of Adam's sin.*

Adam and Eve were also made on day 6

alongside the dinosaurs — so dinosaurs lived with people.

Representatives of all the KINDS of land animals, including the

dinosaur kinds went on board Noah's ark. All those that were left

behind drowned in the cataclysmic circumstances of the flood —

many of their remains became fossils.

Real science can build jet airplanes, make computers, and so on — but real (observational) science cannot deal directly with the past, as we work only in the present. Most people don't realize that evolution is not science — it's a belief about the past.

Creation is not science, either — it's a belief about the past based on the record in the Bible that itself claims to be the ℬord of 𝒢od, *of One who has always existed, and who is perfect and never tells a lie.*

10

If one takes Genesis to Revelation consistently, interpreting Scripture with Scripture, then death and bloodshed of man and animals came into the world only after Adam sinned. The first death of an animal occurred when God shed an animal's blood in the garden and clothed Adam and Eve (Gen. 3:21). This was also a picture of the atonement — symbolic of Christ's blood that was needed to be shed for us.

The King James Bible was first translated in 1611.
Some people think that because the word "dinosaur" is not found in
this or other translations, then the Bible makes no mention of
dinosaurs. However, it wasn't until 1841 that the word
"dinosaur" was first coined!

Genesis 1:21 declares:

"And God created great whales, and every living creature that
moveth, which the waters brought forth abundantly." The Hebrew
word translated "whales" is actually the word for "dragon." In the
first chapter of the first book of the Bible, God is describing His
creation of the great dragons (sea-dwelling dinosaur-like animals.)

Originally, before sin, ALL animals including the dinosaurs were vegetarian. . . . This means that even T. rex, before sin entered the world, ate only plants. . . . Bears have the same sort of teeth structure as a big cat (e.g., lion), but some bears are vegetarian, and others are mainly vegetarian.

14

Many people think that most dinosaurs were large creatures, and thus would never have fit into the ark. But the truth of the matter is that the average size of a dinosaur (based on the skeletons all over the earth) is about the size of a sheep.

And no, *we couldn't clone a dinosaur* even if we had dinosaur DNA as the fictional movie Jurassic Park portrayed — not unless there already was a living female dinosaur. Scientists have found that to clone an animal, they must have an egg of a living female, as there is machinery in the cytoplasm of the egg that is necessary for the creature to develop.

As we read Genesis, we are told how

God took dust and made the first man.

From the man's side He then made the first woman. They were

one flesh. . . . That is why, when a couple is married, the couple

becomes one — it has an historical basis. If Genesis is not true, there

can be no oneness in marriage.

Every single biblical doctrine of theology, directly or indirectly, ultimately has its basis in the Book of Genesis. Therefore, if one does not have a believing understanding of that book (not just believing it is true, but believing and understanding what it says), then one cannot hope to attain full understanding of what Christianity is all about.

18

The universal tendency of things to run down and to fall apart shows that the universe had to be "wound up" at the beginning. It is not eternal. This is totally consistent with "In the beginning God created the heaven and the earth" (Gen. 1:1).

The skeptic asks of Christians, "If God created the universe, then who created God?" But God by definition is *the uncreated Creator* of the universe, so the question "Who created God?" is illogical, just like, "To whom is the bachelor married?"

20

If the days of creation are really "geologic ages" of millions of years, then the gospel message is undermined at its foundation because it puts death, disease, thorns, and suffering before the Fall.

Because God is infinite in power and wisdom,

there's no doubt He could have created the universe and its contents

in no time at all, or six seconds, or six minutes, or six hours

— after all, with God nothing shall be impossible (Luke 1:37).

However, the question to ask is, "Why did God take so long?

Why as long as six days?"

The seven-day week has no basis outside of Scripture.

In this Old Testament passage [Exod. 20:11], God commands

His people, Israel, to work for six days and rest for one — that is

why He deliberately took as long as six days to create everything.

He set the example for man.

As the days of creation are ordinary days in length, then by adding up the years in Scripture (assuming no gaps in the genealogies) the age of the universe is only about six thousand years.

The sun is not needed for day and night! What is needed is light and a rotating earth. On the first day of creation, *God made light* (Gen. 1:3). The phrase "evening and morning" certainly implies a rotating earth. Thus, if we have light from one direction, and a spinning earth, there can be day and night.

Actually, insisting on *six ordinary earth days of creation* is not limiting God, but limiting us to believing that God actually did what He tells us in His Word. Also, if God created everything in six days, like the Bible says, then surely this reveals the power and wisdom of God in a profound way — Almighty God did not need eons of time!

When critics say that Adam could not name the animals in less than one day, what they really mean is they do not understand how they could do it, so Adam could not. However, our brain has suffered from six thousand years of the Curse — it has been greatly affected by the Fall.

Before sin, Adam's brain was perfect.

If we do not allow the language to speak to us in context, but try to make the text fit ideas outside of Scripture, then ultimately the meaning of any word in any part of the Bible depends on man's interpretation — which can change according to whatever outside ideas are in vogue.

For instance, "science" would proclaim that
a person cannot be raised from the dead. Does this mean
we should "interpret" the resurrection of Christ to reflect this?
Sadly, some do just this, saying that the Resurrection simply
means that Jesus' teachings live on in His followers!

Genesis 1:29—30 teaches us that the animals and man were originally created vegetarian. This is consistent with God's description of the creation as *"very good."* How could a fossil record which gives evidence of disease, violence, death, and decay (fossils have been found of animals apparently fighting and certainly eating each other) be described as "very good"?

30

When educators claim they have thrown religion out of the science classroom by eliminating creation, in reality they have thrown Christianity out and replaced it with a new religion — humanism!

Because of intense evolutionary indoctrination, many people today think that our generation is the most intelligent that has ever lived on this planet. But just because we have jet airplanes and computers, it does not mean we are the most intelligent. Modern technology results from the accumulation of knowledge. We stand on the shoulders of those who have gone before us.

What should Christians think about UFO accounts?

. . . Adam's sin caused all of creation to be affected by the Curse,

so why would a race of beings, not of Adam's (sinful) seed,

have their part of creation affected by the Curse,

and then be part of the restoration brought about by Christ,

the last Adam? All of this would seem exceedingly strange.

Eve, in a sense, was a "descendant" of Adam in that she was made from his flesh and thus had some biological connection to him (Gen. 2:21-23). If this were not so, then the gospel could not be explained or defended.

34   *In Genesis 3:20* we read, "And Adam called his wife's name Eve, because she was the mother of all living." In other words, all people other than Adam are descendants of Eve — she was the first woman. This also means Cain's wife was a descendant of Adam. She couldn't have come from another "race" of people and must be accounted for from Adam's descendants.

Cain was in the first generation of children ever born. He (as well as his brothers and sisters) would have received virtually no imperfect genes from Adam or Eve, since the effects of sin and the Curse would have been minimal to start with. In that situation, brother and sister could have married without any potential to produce deformed offspring.

Genesis is the record of the God who was there as history happened.
*It is the **Word of One who knows everything,***
and who is a reliable witness from the past. Thus, when we use
Genesis as a basis for understanding history, we can make sense of
evidence that would otherwise be a real mystery.

Creationists do not believe that God made the animals and plants just as we see them today. For instance, when God made dogs, He didn't make a poodle! After all, dogs like poodles are in fact degenerate mutants, suffering the effects of 6,000 years of the Curse.

38

When Jesus Christ became a man (God-man), He became a descendant of Adam. Thus, He became our relative — totally man, a descendant of the first Adam, yet totally God. Any descendant of Adam can be saved, because our mutual relative by blood (Jesus Christ) died and rose again.

There is really only one race — *the human race.*

Scripture distinguishes people by tribal or national groupings, not by skin color or physical appearances.

The belief that the skin color of black people is a result of a curse on Ham and his descendants is taught **nowhere in the Bible.** *Furthermore, it was not Ham who was cursed; it was his son, Canaan (Gen. 9:18, 25; 10:6), and Canaan's descendants were probably brown-skinned (Gen. 10:15-19).*

Some have claimed that "beasts of the field" mentioned in Genesis actually refers to non-white or "black" people. This is a disgraceful doctrine, and is simply an appeal to prejudice rather than responsible exegesis of the Hebrew, and contradicts the clear teaching that **all people are descended from Adam** *via Noah.*

All the fossils, all the living animals and plants, our planet, the universe — everything exists in the present. We cannot directly test the past using the scientific method (which involves repeating things and watching them happen) since all evidence that we have is in the present.

Creationists base their understanding of creation upon a book which claims to be the Word of the One who was there, who knows everything there is to know about everything, and who tells us what happened. Evolution comes from the words of men who were not there and who do not claim to be omniscient.

Genesis tells us that because of wickedness, God judged the world with a worldwide flood. If this is true, what sort of evidence would we find? We could expect that we would find billions of dead things (fossils) buried in rock layers, laid down by water and catastrophic processes over most of the earth. This is exactly what we observe.

46 *Most cultures have* a story about a worldwide flood similar to Noah's flood. Creation legends — not dissimilar to the account in Genesis regarding the creation of woman, the entrance of death, and the original man and animals being vegetarian (Gen. 1:29–30) — abound in cultures around the world. . . . [These] similarities . . . are not what you would expect from the viewpoint of an evolutionary belief system.

Neither creation nor evolution *can be proven* scientifically.

Surely, as Christians blessed with the conviction that arises from the work of the Holy Spirit, we must accept the Bible as the infallible, authoritative Word of God — otherwise, we have nothing. If the Bible is to be questioned and cannot be trusted, and if it is continually subject to re-interpretation based on what men believe they have discovered, then we do not have an absolute authority.

The real battle is aligned with the fact that these people [evolutionists] do not want to accept Christianity because they will not accept that *there is a God* to whom they are answerable.

50

The public has genuinely been misled into thinking that evolution is only scientific and belief in God is only religious.

You will notice in humanist opposition (through debates, the media, books, etc.) to the creation ministries that they very rarely identify any evidence for evolution. The main reason is, of course, that *there is none*.

It is a shame that creationists do not have *the same media coverage* [as evolutionists] to explain to the world the overwhelming evidence for the truth of creation.

If you are not a Christian, consider these questions: Are you married? Why? Why not just live with someone without bothering to marry? Do you believe marriage is one man for one woman for life? Why not six wives? Or six husbands?

54 *We often hear comments* from parents that their children have rebelled against the Christian ethic, asking why they should obey their parents' rules. One major reason for this is that many Christian parents have not instructed their children from foundational perspectives concerning what they should or should not do. If children see rules as no more than parents' opinions, then why should they obey them?

To understand why living as a homosexual is wrong, one has to understand that the basis for marriage comes from Genesis. It is here we read that *God ordained marriage* and declared it to be one man for one woman for life. God created Adam and Eve, not Adam and Bruce!

Genesis is foundational to the entire Christian philosophy. One major difficulty in our churches is that many people do not trust Genesis. Consequently, they do not know what else in the Bible to trust. They treat the Bible as an interesting book containing some vague sort of religious truth.

57

In the majority of Christian homes today, it is usually the mother who teaches the children spiritually. What an unfortunate thing it is that fathers have not embraced their God-given responsibility. . . . It is the fathers who are allocated the responsibility of providing for their children, and providing the family's spiritual and physical needs.

In Genesis we find that man and animals

were told to eat only plants; they were vegetarians.

Only after the Flood was man told he could eat meat.

There were only vegetarians when God first created,

and there was no violence before Adam sinned.

If you believe in evolution, you must deny a universal paradise before Adam (because you believe that there was death and struggle millions of years before Adam), and also at the end of time (because the Bible teaches the world will be restored to what it used to be). Thus, evolution not only strikes at the heart and the foundation, but at the hope of Christianity as well.

As the creation foundation is removed, we see the godly institutions also start to collapse. On the other hand, as the evolution foundation remains firm, the structures built on that foundation — lawlessness, homosexuality, abortion, etc. — logically increase. We must understand this connection.

In an increasing number of instances, it is apparent that before we can effectively proclaim *the message of Christ* we must establish the creation foundation upon which the rest of the gospel can be built.

62

Throughout the Old and New Testament, *Genesis is quoted* from or referred to more than any other book in the entire Bible.

We have absolutely no idea where the Garden of Eden was located. . . . We need to remember that the whole world was destroyed by the flood of Noah's day. The Garden of Eden would have also been destroyed. During the Flood, the continents probably split apart, forming a totally different-looking earth to that before the Flood.

Why did Adam get the blame when Eve was the one who took the first bite of the forbidden fruit? . . . When you read Genesis, you find that it was Adam who was given the specific instruction not to eat the fruit of the tree. You see, Adam was created first, and God had ordained that he was to be the head of his family. . . . Adam, of course, would have told Eve, because she was really under his headship.

Why do some Christians insist that Noah's flood was a local event? The main reason is because they've accepted the evolutionists' teaching that the fossil record is millions of years old. They recognize that a global flood would destroy such a record and lay down a new one.

66

Noah didn't need to take all the species of land animals on board — just representatives of the kinds. . . . Calculations show that probably only around 16,000 animals were needed on board the ark.

Sadly, when these children then go to a public educational institution and are taught the foundation of evolution, many reject Christianity and the structure collapses. Many parents have noticed that the decline in their children's interest in Christianity went hand in hand with increasing levels of education in public schools, colleges, etc.

When the *"windows of heaven were opened,"* this produced rain on the earth for 40 days and 40 nights. There must've been much more water vapor in the atmosphere before the Flood, because if all the water vapor in our present atmosphere fell as rain, the ground would be covered to an average depth of less than two inches.

There are those in the Church who believe that Noah's flood

was just a local event — not a global catastrophe. However,

God gave the covenant of the rainbow

as a sign He would never again flood the earth as He did in

Noah's day. . . . Now if Noah's flood was just a local event, then

this means God did not keep His promise!

70

I've had lots of people over the years say that *if we could only find Noah's ark,* then we could convince people the Bible's true. But you know what? Even though it would be a great find, I personally don't believe this would convince many people to believe the Bible.

Scientists have been interested in the canyons they've seen on Mars. In fact, they believe these canyons were formed by the action of water. . . . I had to smile when I read this. You see, the majority of scientists don't believe a flood of biblical proportions occurred on earth — which is mostly covered by water. Yet these same scientists believe there was a massive flood on Mars — which has no water!

Over the years, I've often listened to people talk about the supposed curse of Ham. Sadly, I've also heard some people, including some Christian leaders, claim that this curse resulted in the black-skinned people being formed. *Frankly, this is nonsense.*

Because of the influence of evolutionary ideas, which have popularized Neanderthal man as a less-than-human caveman, most people think cavemen have something to do with evolution. . . . However, when Noah's descendants started spreading out over the earth after the Tower of Babel, some people would have used caves for shelter. This doesn't mean they were primitive — they just used the best shelter they could find before most of them would eventually build homes.

73

74

At the end of the Flood, because of volcanic action and continental movement, the oceans would have been warm and the land cool. Ash in the atmosphere would have blocked out sunlight, also causing a cooling effect. Therefore, lots of water would have evaporated, and then precipitated in the form of ice and snow — causing an ice age.

Actually, did you know that representatives of every kind of animal that God created once lived in the Middle East? . . . *The Bible tells us* that a man called Noah built an ark to save him, his family, and representatives of all the kinds of land animals during the global flood God sent as a judgment. And where did this ark land after the Flood? In the mountains of Ararat — the land known today as the Middle East.

Because people have been brainwashed by evolutionary teaching, many Christians insist that Genesis is not important to the gospel. I've even had many pastors tell me that the most important thing is that people trust in Jesus and it doesn't matter whether they believe in Genesis or not. . . . Original sin is foundational to the gospel. Churches need to be teaching the gospel starting with Genesis.

Constantly people tell me that the days of creation can't be six literal days because scientists have proved that the earth is billions of years old. *Actually, they haven't shown that at all.* You see, dating methods have all sorts of assumptions built into their equations by scientists who are fallible men who weren't there at the beginning.

78

In October of 1953, National Geographic *magazine published a photograph of a bat that had fallen on a stalagmite in the famous Carlsbad Caverns in New Mexico. The stalagmite had grown so fast, it was able to preserve the bat before it decomposed. Obviously, this didn't take millions of years!*

A religion can be defined as a concept, or principle or system of belief, held to with ardor and faith. This is exactly what evolution is. . . . But it's also a religion of death. Evolution teaches that death existed from the beginning. The deaths of billions of creatures over billions of years finally led to man. When a person dies — that's the end of them. . . . But . . . when we die, we live forever — with God or without Him. That's why Jesus Christ came to die — so we might *live forever with Him!*

Now I call this tree of the knowledge of good and evil the "tree of death." This is because if Adam ate from it, then death would enter the world. In a real sense, Adam had a choice — the tree of life or the tree of death. Sadly, he chose the tree of death. That's why there is death all around us. It is a judgment from a Holy God because of sin.

People have been shocked in recent times
at the outbreaks of school violence in America. . . . I believe
what we see happening is the outworking of an education system
that has eliminated God from the classroom. When you think about
it, generations of young people are being brainwashed each day in
evolutionary ideas. They're being told that they're nothing special —
they're just animals that have evolved from some lower form of
animal over millions of years.

81

82

Now, a bellybutton is actually the scar of where a person was once connected by the umbilical cord to their mother. Adam and Eve would not have had such a scar because they were made as mature human beings — they weren't ever connected by an umbilical cord.

Notice that in explaining why Jesus died, Paul went to the Book of Genesis and its account of Adam and the Fall. In other words, one cannot really understand the good news in the New Testament of Jesus' death and resurrection, and thus payment for sin, until one understands the bad news in Genesis of the fall of man, and thus the origin of sin and its penalty of death.

As Christians,

we need to answer this question: Is it essential to believe

in a literal Fall? Absolutely! If there was no literal Fall,

then what is sin? Who defines it?

Young people today have little or no understanding of what is meant by sin or of its consequences. They are growing up in a culture that teaches them they are just evolved animals and that there is no Creator God to whom they are accountable. Logically, then, there is no basis for absolutes, and everyone has a right to their own opinions; there must be a tolerance of all views (although Christianity is considered intolerant, because it is exclusive).

86

Many people today have the wrong idea about evolution.
They think Charles Darwin invented this theory. But this is
simply not true. Darwin did popularize a particular view
of evolution, but *evolutionary ideas go
way back in history.*

Now, don't get me wrong here. People are not stupid. They are just being consistent with their presuppositions. Hitler was not silly. Some even say in some ways he was a genius, albeit he was warped in his thinking. But he consistently applied what he believed about origins. This led to the deaths of millions of people. Abortionists today are not intellectually inferior. They are just being consistent with their presuppositions, the foundation they ultimately have for their thinking.

I'm not saying that evolution is the cause of abortion or school violence. *What I am saying is that the more a culture abandons God's Word as the absolute authority, and the more a culture accepts an evolutionary philosophy, then the way people think, and their attitudes, will also change. I'm not saying that a student says to himself,* Now, I'm just an animal — I know evolution is true — therefore there's no basis for right or wrong — so there's nothing to stop me from shooting my teacher. *But what has happened is that the thinking of generations of people has gradually changed so that they don't think in a Christian framework anymore.*

The first verse in the first book of the Bible states: *"In the beginning God created the heaven and the earth."* God, who has always existed (no one made God, for He made everything), tells us in this first verse that He made time ("beginning"), space ("heaven"), and matter ("earth").

We do know what T. rex ate originally — and it wasn't animals or people. It was plants. . . . Adam and Eve (and all the animals) were told they were only to eat plants for food. They were all vegetarian.

When it came to the very few dinosaur kinds that grew to a very large size, God probably sent "teenagers," NOT "fully grown adults" on the ark.

Some people argue, "But there were too many dinosaurs to fit on the ark." Although scientists have made up over 600 names of dinosaurs, there were probably less than 50 actual kinds of dinosaurs.

When you think about it, if animals and plants that die are just left on the ground, they decay into dust. To form a fossil of an animal or plant, they must be covered by lots of mud very quickly, or they'll just disappear. To form millions of fossils in layers that are miles thick in places over the earth, there had to have been enormous amounts of water and mud. What does this sound like? Noah's flood, of course!

93

94

*Many people think that most fossils are millions of years old. Remember, however, that there was **no death of animals or people before sin**. As Noah's flood occurred about 4,500 ago, that means the fossils from the flood are only 4,500 years old.*

Actually, we DO know what happened to the dinosaurs! Because of sin, the Curse, and the Flood, we now have such things as famines, droughts, floods, fire, diseases, people killing animals, and animals killing each other. In other words, the same reasons that animals become extinct today, are the SAME reasons that dinosaurs died out. And it wasn't millions of years ago; it was probably just hundreds of years ago. *There is no mystery whatsoever.*

By the way, if evolution were true, you would expect to find in the fossil record evidence of in-between or transitional forms, as one kind of animal changed into a totally different kind of animal. *But you don't find any such things!* Dinosaurs, for instance, have always been dinosaurs.

If there's so much evidence for the Flood all over the earth, and if it's so obvious God created, and the Bible is true, wouldn't the scientists surely believe these things? The answer is that scientists, like everyone else, are sinners. Because of this, they don't want to believe. It has nothing to do with the evidence. There is an exception, of course, for those whose hearts have been changed by the Holy Spirit, becoming true Christians.

98 To start with, it must be understood that *evolution is really not science.* In fact, it is plain straight religion. The average Christian doesn't seem to understand that. Ask the average person the question "What is science?" and try to get them to write down a definition! Most couldn't do this. If you don't know what science is and what it isn't, then how do you know whether scientists are being scientific in what they say?

All fossils exist in the present.

When scientists dig up fossils, they are not digging up the PAST but the PRESENT. When you observe fossils, you are observing evidence that exists in the present. The pictures the scientists draw to explain the fossils are only a story (conjecture). They did not see the organisms living.

Evolution can be defined as a belief about the past based on the words of scientists who don't know everything, who were not there, and who are trying to explain how the evidence, which only exists in the present, got there.

Genesis is foundational in understanding science and history. However, the Book of Genesis is one of the most disbelieved and attacked books in both Christian and non-Christian circles.

For a free catalog or for more information about what the Bible teaches, contact one of the Answers in Genesis ministries below.

Answers in Genesis
P.O. Box 6330
Florence, KY 41022
USA

Answers in Genesis
P.O. Box 6302
Acacia Ridge DC
QLD 4110
Australia

Answers in Genesis
5-420 Erb St. West
Suite 213
Waterloo, Ontario
Canada N2L 6K6

Answers in Genesis
P.O. Box 39005
Howick, Auckland
New Zealand

Answers in Genesis
P.O. Box 5262
Leicester LE2 3XU
United Kingdom

Answers in Genesis
Attn: Nao Hanada
3317-23 Nagaoka, Ibaraki-machi
Higashi-ibaraki-gun, Ibaraki-ken
    311-3116
Japan

In addition, you may contact:
        Institute for Creation Research
        P.O. Box 2667
        El Cajon, CA 92021

Other Offerings by Ken Ham

A Is for Adam, with Mally Ham (Green Forest, AR: Master Books, 1995). Also available on CD-Rom.

Answers . . . with Ken Ham, 3-volume DVD set (Green Forest, AR: Master Books, 2002).

The Answers Book, with Andrew Snelling and Carl Wieland (Green Forest, AR: Master Books, 1990).

Did Adam Have a Bellybutton? (Green Forest, AR: Master Books, 2000).

Did Eve Really Have an Extra Rib? (Green Forest, AR: Master Books, 2002).

Dinosaurs of Eden (Green Forest, AR: Master Books, 2001).

D Is for Dinosaur, with Mally Ham (Green Forest, AR: Master Books, 1991). Video also available.

Genesis and the Decay of the Nations (Green Forest, AR: Master Books, 1991).

The Great Dinosaur Mystery Solved (Green Forest, AR: Master Books, 1998).

The Lie: Evolution (Green Forest, AR: Master Books, 1987).

One Blood, with Don Batten and Carl Wieland (Green Forest, AR: Master Books, 1999).

The Relevance of Creation (Green Forest, AR: Master Books, 1988).

Walking Through Shadows, with Carl Wieland (Green Forest, AR: Master Books, 2002).

What Really Happened to the Dinosaurs? with John D. Morris (Green Forest, AR: Master Books, 1990).

When Christians Roamed the Earth, with various other authors (Green Forest, AR: Master Books, 2001).

Why Won't They Listen? (Green Forest, AR: Master Books, 2002).

Ken Ham is one of the most in-demand Christian conference speakers in the United States. He is the executive director of Answers in Genesis and the author of many books emphasizing the relevance of the Book of Genesis to the lives of people.

one hundred one SIGNS *of* DESIGN